I0420581

Quote Octopus
Melbourne, Victoria, 3053
Australia
www.quoteoctopus.com

Congratulations!

Follow Quote Octopus on Social Media for FREE Books And the Chance to Win Incredible Daily Prizes!

Facebook.com/QuoteOctopus

Twitter.com/QuoteOctopus

Youtube.com/QuoteOctopus

A computer once beat me at chess, but it was no match for me at kick boxing.

Emo Philips

Mental strength is really important because you either win or lose in your mind. And I'm not solely talking about sporting matches, boxing events - anything you do, you do it first with your mental strength. And you can actually train and develop it, and I am responsible for what I'm saying because I have experience with that.

Wladimir Klitschko

Boxing is the only sport you can get your brain shook, your money took and your name in the undertaker book.

Joe Frazier

Sonny Liston is nothing. The man can't talk. The man can't fight. The man needs talking lessons. The man needs boxing lessons. And since he's gonna fight me, he needs falling lessons.

Muhammad Ali

It's less about the physical training, in the end, than it is about the mental preparation: boxing is a chess game. You have to be skilled enough and have trained hard enough to know how many different ways you can counterattack in any situation, at any moment.

Jimmy Smits

I'm a satirist, so I've got boxing gloves on if the person is worthy of satire. But I'm not an assassin. If that ever happens, it's only because something happened during the interview that got me going, and then I had to translate my feelings to the mouth of the character.

Stephen Colbert

All of my life had been spent in the shadow of apartheid. And when South Africa went through its extraordinary change in 1994, it was like having spent a lifetime in a boxing ring with an opponent and suddenly finding yourself in that boxing ring with nobody else and realising you've to take the gloves off and get out, and reinvent yourself.

Athol Fugard

Never give up, which is the lesson I learned from boxing. As soon as you learn to never give up, you have to learn the power and wisdom of unconditional surrender, and that one doesn't cancel out the other; they just exist as contradictions. The wisdom of it comes as you get older.

Kris Kristofferson

People don't realize what they had till it's gone. Like President Kennedy, there was no one like him, the Beatles, and my man Elvis Presley. I was the Elvis of boxing.

Muhammad Ali

In boxing, I had a lot of fear. Fear was good. But, for the first time, in the bout with Muhammad Ali, I didn't have any fear. I thought, 'This is easy. This is what I've been waiting for'. No fear at all. No nervousness. And I lost.

George Foreman

I grew up with an impatience with the anti-scientific. So I'm a bit miffed with our current love affair with all things Eastern. If I sneeze on the set, 40 people hand me echinacea. But I'd no sooner take that than eat a pencil. Maybe that's why I took up boxing. It's my response to men in white pajamas feeling each other's chi.

Hugh Laurie

Boxing is not about your feelings. It's about performance.

Manny Pacquiao

All the time he's boxing, he's thinking. All the time he was thinking, I was hitting him.

Jack Dempsey

All that is worth seeing in good boxing can best be witnessed in a contest with soft gloves. Every value is called out: quickness, force, precision, foresight, readiness, pluck, and endurance. With these, the rowdy and 'rough' are not satisfied.

John Boyle O'Reilly

My husband and I went to Bald Head Island for our four-year anniversary. We spent the night in bed with champagne, tequila and Krispy Kreme doughnuts and watched a boxing match on Showtime.

Teri Polo

Boxing is a sport. We allow each other to hit each other, but I'm not treating my opponent like my enemy. We're doing a job to entertain people.

Manny Pacquiao

Reality show? You can't find anything better than boxing because of the trials and errors, the ups and downs, the struggle when you get knocked down to get back up. Use it symbolically and interchangeably for life.

Don King

I was a tiger, a good fighter, in good shape, but I was always nervous before boxing matches.

George Foreman

Boxing is a lot of white men watching two black men beat each other up.

Muhammad Ali

Boxing should focus on pitting champion versus champion - those are the fights that everyone wants to see. The sports also needs to work on developing new heroes and personalities. I'd like to see more vignettes on fighters, focusing on their lives, goals and stories. Boxers need to be larger than life.

Sugar Ray Leonard

Fighting and everything I have done has been a political statement throughout my career. Boxing is life. It is the closest thing to life you can get. It is man-to-man. You can't call a time out or get a substitute. If you run out of gas, there is no petrol station around. Your problem is right before you, and you have to deal with it. That is life.

Don King

We all think we've got one more boxing match in us, and that, probably, will be the downfall of Floyd Mayweather, George Foreman, Manny Pacquiao. We'll overstay our welcome.

George Foreman

Boxing is a celebration of the lost religion of masculinity all the more trenchant for its being lost.

Joyce Carol Oates

Boxing is a sport, but it's also entertainment. I wanted to transcend the sport and be considered just not as a fighter, or a champion, but someone very special.

Sugar Ray Leonard

I have been so great in boxing they had to create an image like Rocky, a white image on the screen, to counteract my image in the ring. America has to have its white images, no matter where it gets them. Jesus, Wonder Woman, Tarzan and Rocky.

Muhammad Ali

I've been on the opposite side of decisions before when the crowd would be booing and saying that I lost. I've lived with it. Judging in boxing has been same since the beginning, and it isn't gonna change.

George Foreman

I think I've become one of the best finishers in boxing; if I hurt a guy, I normally take him out.

Sugar Ray Leonard

I was painfully initiated into boxing, because the guys I fought were a lot bigger than me.

Sugar Ray Leonard

My mother gave me boxing gloves; I wanted boxing gloves. I liked to box. So I still have them. They're still in my bookcase, very old, tattered, and they were cherished.

Pierce Brosnan

I enjoy the school run and being a dad. Boxing will always be with me. I like that.

Sugar Ray Leonard

The boxing game has been good, so we need to give back. We have to teach young men how to be men.

Joe Frazier

I'm one of the most optimistic persons in the world. I always believed that - there's another shot, another chance. In boxing, I never gave up. I kept trying, kept trying. Even when things seemed so dim, I continued to push forward to make something happen in my favor.

Sugar Ray Leonard

I'm the worst surfer in California. My balance is off from boxing.

Mickey Rourke

I've always boxed, I always taught boxing.

Adam Carolla

When I'm boxing, if my career isn't going well, at least I feel mentally and physically strong.

Liam Hemsworth

The opportunity and the concept of merging music culture with actual boxing is exciting. It's bringing a younger demographic to the sport.

Curtis Jackson

Well, of course a boxing match is hard because boxing isn't set for you to do good. You have to force your will upon someone, but dancing you don't have to force your will. It should be a lot easier because if I make a mistake I don't get hit.

Evander Holyfield

In boxing, you get hit, it's painful, then you sit on the stool when the adrenaline is gone and you feel that pain. And then you fight the next round.

Ben Horowitz

It is up to the people and boxing fans to give me the respect I deserve once I have finished my career. I personally do not think about my legacy.

Wladimir Klitschko

I like boxing.

Marion Barry

When I came into boxing, I brought it to the next level with adverts and doing pantomime and people just got jealous of me doing that.

Frank Bruno

My trainer, George Francis, used to train a lot of African boxers. They're hungry guys, man. They've got no trainers, got nothing. They're so hungry to do boxing, to make some money.

Frank Bruno

Boxing has kept me off the streets, stops me smoking and drinking and gives me something to do.

Billy Joe Saunders

Boxing is my real passion. I can go to ballet, theatre, movies, or other sporting events... and nothing is like the fights to me. I'm excited by the visual beauty of it. A boxer can look so spectacular by doing a good job.

LeRoy Neiman

I've been a boxing fan ever since I was a kid.

Robert Goulet

Barney was interested in bringing professional boxing back to Northern Ireland in a big way.

Barry McGuigan

I put my money in property and I love merchandise; such as Muhammad Ali boxing gloves. It's about stability for the future.

Shayne Ward

Boxing is one of the few sports that is one on one.

Irwin Winkler

I'm back in Boston. I own an outdoor deck hockey rink, and I own a boxing gym here also.

Micky Ward

I know my Beijing medal has been a watershed moment in the history of Indian boxing , but personally speaking, I would like to better it in London.

Vijender Singh

I've grown up with Bollywood, and I continue to enjoy it. But boxing remains my passion.

Vijender Singh

But I did a lot of boxing and I was captain of an Australian surf club.

Rod Taylor

Everything in our family was always boxing. It was the life my father chose for me.

Nonito Donaire

I was 11 when I started boxing. My brother was fighting before I did, and he got me into it.

Nonito Donaire

I'm a big fan of the 'Rocky' series. Given the chance, I'd love to meet Sylvester Stallone. But apart from boxing, I'm an ardent fan of tennis and football.

Vijender Singh

If at my funeral they're talking about my boxing stories, I'd be disappointed because this is just a springboard for when I'm finished. It's just a game. It's pretty silly when you think about it: two grown men punching each other in the face and taking it seriously.

Mark de Mori

One of my all-time favorite workouts is boxing.

Cassie Scerbo

I love boxing. I like to see the strategizing. Watching the warriors go to work. I like that struggle, going out there and fighting.

Barry Larkin

Putting prize-fighting altogether aside as one of the unavoidable evils attending on this manly exercise, the inestimable value of boxing as a training, discipline, and development of boys and young men remains.

John Boyle O'Reilly

Boxing is changing and training methods are slowly being dragged into the 21st century.

Barry McGuigan

Boxing traditionally was received very well and accepted on both sides.

Barry McGuigan

I've never boxed before in my life. I've had one day's training at a boxing gym, and it's an incredibly difficult sport.

Rupert Penry-Jones

To recognize that head injuries were as essential a part of football as they are of boxing would be to erase the fine distinction on which the game's respectability rested.

Charlie Pierce

I'm just a seasonal guy. Basketball, football, baseball, boxing, golf. Give it to me all the time.

Jerry Ferrara

Boxing should probably be banned. But until then, I'm a big fan.

Sam Simon

Later in July I'm going to be promoting and putting on a boxing show of amateur fighters from July 21st through the 28th where one hundred kids will be fighting and competing with each other to see who's going to be the best.

Alexis Arguello

Any big televised event that starts at the crack of dawn is worth getting up for. I've done it all my life: big boxing matches, royal weddings, even TV-A.M.'s inaugural episode was enjoyed in pyjamas in my house.

Sharon Horgan

As a West Side kid fooling around with boxing gloves, I had been, for some reason of temperament, more interested in dodging a blow than in striking one.

Gene Tunney

I love boxing, MMA, and hiking with my dog. I work out 3 times a week, and on my off days, I do yoga to keep my body relaxed and to stretch.

Natalie Martinez

Jagdish Singh was my basic coach, and he trained me from my very early days in boxing, teaching me the fundamentals of the sport. He was the one who shaped me into a boxer, disciplined me when I required disciplining.

Vijender Singh

My favorite television show of all time is 'Hill Street Blues.' I think it's the show that is to television what Pele was to football or Muhammad Ali was to boxing.

Lennie James

I think on balance, Don King has been bad for boxing. I think he's done some very good things and I think he did a heck of a job of promoting Ali but I think I could have promoted Ali.

Dick Schaap

Even while modeling, I was still practicing kung fu and boxing as sports.

Djimon Hounsou

I earned a black belt when I was in high school. And I did a lot of boxing and full contact karate in college.

Dean Norris

I was training in Gleason's Gym on 30th and 8th Avenue, where it was the Mecca of boxing, and a guy walked in who couldn't rub two quarters together and said, 'Did you ever think of being on TV?' And somehow I ended up in 'Taxi,' which is the craziest thing of all.

Tony Danza

Sugar Ray wouldn't give me a rematch, and that's the reason I walked away from boxing.

Marvin Hagler

I don't want to sound obnoxious, but I like to think I brought it another step. I was able to bring people who were casually interested in boxing together.

Barry McGuigan

I think it's fair to say I've always been a boxing fan.

Walter Hill

I've always wanted to do a boxing movie.

Walter Hill

Once or twice a week, I try to do some kind of boxing. I'm hitting the bags and jumping rope - all that stuff.

Mekhi Phifer

Boxing is always serious. Nothing comical or funny about boxing.

Juan Manuel Marquez

I started boxing when I was eight. Me and my brother Rafael started boxing in amateur tournaments when I was 13. My father was an ex-pro boxer.

Juan Manuel Marquez

There's such a big buzz around boxing at the moment. Everything's happening and there's so much building up with a lot of young talent coming through.

Billy Joe Saunders

In boxing, everybody has their favorites.

Thomas Hearns

The debate analysis in the media is rampant with contest analogies of war, baseball, boxing, football; you name it. Any testosterone contest imaginable is fair game.

Jonathan Raymond

My fighting style, if you will, is a combination of mimicking, cowboy films and boxing that I have done throughout my life.

Dominic Purcell

I like doing very high action things. Running, boxing, a lot of free weights. They're not heavy. I eat what I want, really, because I think that while you're working out you can eat better.

Natasha Bedingfield

Baseball, boxing, handball - sooner or later every game gets compared to narrative, but only in football are the plays perfectly linear, drawn up with letters, and only in football is the field itself lined like a sheet of notebook paper.

J. R. Moehringer

My dad just wanted me to find something to do to keep me out of trouble. Boxing was the great escape.

Diego Corrales

Even though I had been boxing, I had no idea I could beat somebody in the ring. And I had no idea I could really take a punch. When I realized that, I really started taking off.

Cara Castronuova

Maybe with boxing and good focus, I can fix myself and make my mother proud.

Amnat Ruenroeng

As everyone in boxing knows, styles makes fights.

Miguel Cotto

Some say Hollywood movies that are made about boxing are just metaphors for other things, I think I've made one that's actually about boxing and not a metaphor.

Walter Hill

I love the whole world of boxing and the sense of community that exists there.

Holt McCallany

Kids will come into my boxing gym with no discipline, and then you teach them how to focus and love what they're doing, which then travels outside into their home and work life.

Tamer Hassan

Boxing is doing OK in Australia, but there isn't much money here. I hear guys are paid three grand for an Australian title, and there is no career in that. My goal has always been the big time, and that's America. I grew up idolising Mike Tyson and Evander Holyfield and, for me, it was always Vegas and Don King with his crazy hair and waving flags.

Mark de Mori

I don't want to be named myself as one of the elite boxers of Puerto Rico. That's for the fans and for the people that know about boxing. I just want to do my job the best I can, and I am going to do that the rest of my career.

Miguel Cotto

I was like any other kid: very normal, I can say. I just was a simple kid that came from a humble family and was taught by my father to be a family man and be committed to them. I stepped into boxing following my older brothers.

Miguel Cotto

My team members are Hector Soto, who is a boxing promoter and Vice-president of Miguel Cotto Promotions. He runs all my business. He was the person that my father left in charge of it all. Bryan Perez is my right-hand man.

Miguel Cotto

Some of our best fighters are not only Puerto Rican greats but all-time greats of the sport. Carlos Ortiz, Wilfredo Gomez, Wilfredo Benitez and Felix 'Tito' Trinidad and many others have made Puerto Rican boxing what it is today, and I am only an extension of their greatness.

Miguel Cotto

What people don't know is that I'm a blackbelt in jujitsu, which I've been for 20 years, and I've been boxing since I've been 15 years old - those are things that come natural to me.

Frank Grillo

For the last years now I've had my own academy where I train Brazilian Jujitsu and Tae boxing, Muay Thai everyday.

Sean Patrick Flanery

As soon as I get time, I want to start to do some fight training. I tried a little boxing once with my personal trainer back in L.A. - it's such a good workout, and it's a good skill to have, especially in my industry, since sometimes you have to do stunts and fight scenes.

Katia Winter

Boxing's not a career for anyone: it doesn't last long enough to be a career.

Chris Penn

I ran into a couple of guys who were boxers. They talked me into working out at their gym. I became obsessed with boxing and the idea of becoming a champion.

Jon Seda

I thought boxing was stupid.

John G. Avildsen

It's a lot tougher to play soccer and make it look believable. But in boxing, it was easier for me. I got injured a lot more in the soccer world. In soccer, I pulled muscles. I thought boxing was going to be tougher.

Kuno Becker

All of the sports have a safety net, but boxing is the only sport that has none. So when the fighter is through, he is through. While he was fighting his management was very excited for him, but now that he is done, that management team is moving on.

Gerry Cooney

I am the astronaut of boxing. Joe Louis and Dempsey were just jet pilots. I'm in a world of my own.

Muhammad Ali

I've seen George Foreman shadow boxing, and the shadow won.

Muhammad Ali

Boxing brings out my aggressive instinct, not necessarily a killer instinct.

Sugar Ray Leonard

I was not athletically inclined. I was very quiet, introverted, non-confrontational. My three older brothers were athletes - basketball, football - but I was kind of a momma's boy. Then one day, my brother Roger encouraged me to go to the boxing gym with him. I tried the gloves on, and it just felt so natural.

Sugar Ray Leonard

Boxing is the ultimate challenge. There's nothing that can compare to testing yourself the way you do every time you step in the ring.

Sugar Ray Leonard

Boxing gave me the opportunities to grow into the person that I am today.

Alexis Arguello

Boxing is the ultimate challenge. There's nothing that can compare to testing yourself the way you do every time you step in the ring. On the downside, you meet a lot of really bad people in boxing, at all stages of your career.

Sugar Ray Leonard

Wrestling and boxing is like Ping-Pong and rugby. There's no connection.

Mickey Rourke

I'm a satirist, so I've got boxing gloves on if the person is worthy of satire. But I'm not an assassin.

Stephen Colbert

I think my grandmother saw my potential first. When I was young, I told her, 'I think I should get a job.' She said, 'No, just keep boxing.'

Floyd Mayweather, Jr.

A boxing match is like a cowboy movie. There's got to be good guys and there's got to be bad guys. And that's what people pay for - to see the bad guys get beat.

Sonny Liston

I see the beauty in boxing. It teaches me strength physically, but mostly mentally. I had to learn my strength, because for so long I could have been tougher than I was.

Kelly Rowland

I don't promote boxing, I promote people. Boxing is a catalyst to bring people together.

Don King

In boxing you create a strategy to beat each new opponent, it's just like chess.

Lennox Lewis

Boxing is real easy. Life is much harder.

Floyd Mayweather, Jr.

Boxing is about being hit rather more than it is about hitting, just as it is about feeling pain, if not devastating psychological paralysis, more than it is about winning.

Joyce Carol Oates

I've had boxing gloves on since before I could walk and been in gyms all of my life.

Floyd Mayweather, Jr.

Boxing was not something I truly enjoyed. Like a lot of things in life, when you put the gloves on, it's better to give than to receive.

Sugar Ray Leonard

People say it's a movie about boxing, but... I don't agree at all. I don't think it's a movie about boxing. Boxing is like a platform. It's just a stage where this is played out.

Morgan Freeman

I like very much to ride horses. I like soccer, I have had a passion for boxing since I was a child, although it would be stupid for me to box.

Andrea Bocelli

The boxing world is full of all kinds of corruption.

Al Sharpton

There are a lot of things and in order to be at the top and maintain your focus you have to have something that motivates you. For me, it was what I perceived as a lack of respect from the boxing world as well as the media, which made me want to work so hard and be great.

Marvin Hagler

My goal is not getting hit and to knock the other guy out. Some people might complain because they want to see boxers beat up on each other, but you cannot last long in professional boxing if you take a lot of punches.

Wladimir Klitschko

Since I was a boy of five or six, I had it in my mind I would be a world boxing champion.

Joe Frazier

I want to be remembered as a great athlete. As a boxing champion.

Idi Amin

To say what I would have been if I wasn't boxing, I don't know why, but I always wanted to be an x-ray technician or a substitute teacher. Those two occupations always stuck with me, maybe because my substitute teacher didn't give us homework, or because I've always had x-rays of my hands.

Sugar Ray Leonard

It's kind of ironic that the two sports with the greatest characters, boxing and horse racing, have both been on the decline. In both cases it's for the lack of a suitable hero.

Dick Schaap

My father taught me, in boxing, that when you - particularly when you get hit in the face for the first time - you're going to panic. That instead of panicking, just accept it. Stay calm. And any time anybody hits you, they always leave themselves open to be hit.

Rudy Giuliani

I developed that for a long time. I also developed 'Sugar Sweet Science' at New Line and that didn't happen. That was a boxing movie. And between all that there were a couple of other things.

Danny DeVito

James Franco is a Method actor. I respect Method actors, but he never snapped out of character. Whenever we'd have to get in the ring for boxing scenes, and even during practice, the dude was full-on hitting me.

Tyrese Gibson

In boxing you never know who you're going to face in ring.

Manny Pacquiao

I run, but boxing conditioning is different, so you have to get used to running in the ring. Boxing movements are very different. Swimming is one of the best because every single muscle is working. I swim a lot. I train very hard at things that mimic boxing. I have to do mostly sport-specific training, such as lots of sparring.

Wladimir Klitschko

I've fought everybody without ducking anyone. I have beaten 10 undefeated guys, and I never was comparing myself to the greatest in the sport. I was not thinking of breaking any records. I'm just enjoying my time in boxing.

Wladimir Klitschko

Without boxing, I can't live. I love boxing.

Mary Kom

When archaeologists discover the missing arms of Venus de Milo, they will find she was wearing boxing gloves.

John Barrymore

Boxing is sort of an inevitability. We know they are going to be pounding each other.

Sylvester Stallone

Boxing is like jazz. The better it is, the less people appreciate it.

George Foreman

My father was an army champion boxer... in the British army. And so he loved boxing and talked it up as a sport. But then when my brother and I were beating the crap out of each other, he was always trying to tone it down. But I am a fan of boxing.

Hugh Jackman

Aside from a handful of guys boxing is missing the good trainers, that's why our sport is so in the air now because we don't have people who have the capability to not only train fighters but also train and create decent respectable citizens of the world.

Alexis Arguello

I've always loved boxing. It's something I've always been extremely excited about.

Louis C. K.

The content and thematic materials of dance is, of itself, like boxing. You play tennis and baseball. But boxing is not a sport you play: you stand up and do it.

Twyla Tharp

I wanted to be the best street fighter in Houston, Texas. And I thought if I got a trophy or two, I'd go back home, and everyone would be afraid of me. I had one fight in '67, the first one. In '68 of October, I was an Olympic gold-medalist, a dream come true, with a total of 25 boxing matches.

George Foreman

Boxing has become America's tragic theater.

Joyce Carol Oates

A boxing workout is the heaviest thing, but it's the best. The worst part is that boxing gyms are the smelliest things in the universe. You have to lie down on the floor, where everyone has been sweating and spitting, and do 1,000 situps and push-ups.

Gael Garcia Bernal

I was drawn to boxing because I got beat up as a kid. I was the kid with the piano books in a New York neighbourhood.

Billy Joel

Boxing is the toughest and loneliest sport in the world. You've got all the fans, lots of hangers-on jumping up and shouting different words. But when you actually go in the ring, it's a very lonely and scary place. It's just you and the other guy.

Frank Bruno

I love boxing. There's something fierce about using your body's force that way.

Sophia Bush

I've seen George Foreman shadow boxing and the shadow won.

George Foreman

I knew boxing before I knew anything else.

Floyd Mayweather, Jr.

Muhammad Ali was a god, an idol and an icon. He was boxing. Any kid that had the opportunity to talk to Ali, to get advice from Muhammad Ali, was privileged. He's always given me time to ask questions, although I was so in awe that I didn't ask questions.

Sugar Ray Leonard

Boxing was the only career where I wouldn't have to start out at the bottom. I had a good resume.

Sugar Ray Leonard

There's ups and downs with boxing, layoffs are part of the sport and they can either help or hurt a guy.

Floyd Mayweather, Jr.

People are hurt in love affairs and never recover, more than a boxing match.

George Foreman

When I left boxing in 1977 to be a preacher, I couldn't make a fist after I learned about Jesus Christ.

George Foreman

I always put my boxing first.

Floyd Mayweather, Jr.

I hope to have one more boxing match at the age of 55. Given that demographic at the age of 55 to 65, you've got to make a statement with your life. Otherwise, you are just existing.

George Foreman

You don't appreciate things until they're gone. For me, I miss my friends; I don't miss boxing, I miss the camaraderie.

Sugar Ray Leonard

Boxing is what pays my bills.

Floyd Mayweather, Jr.

I started a youth center in Houston. The kids would come in and want to learn to box; they wanted to tear up the world, beat up the world. And I'd try to show them they didn't need anger. They didn't need all that killing instinct they'd read about. You can be a human being and pursue boxing as a sport.

George Foreman

Boxing is individual, although there's a team concept because you need a great corner, you need a great trainer, you need a great prep man, you need all of these things, but it's more of a Mano a Mano; it's more you versus me. I miss that time in training camp and Dad and Mom cooking meals. It was one big family.

Sugar Ray Leonard

Boxing's a poor man's sport. We can't afford to play golf or tennis. It is what it is. It's kept so many kids off the street. It kept me off the street.

Sugar Ray Leonard

Boxing has been the most difficult thing I've ever done. The biggest challenge in my life. I was a boxer. That was hard. Everything else is pretty easy.

George Foreman

I always expect unexpected challenges. Boxing is not an easy sport.

Sugar Ray Leonard

For the most part, I think video games do a good job of capturing the essence of boxing. However, I'd like to continue to see them push the realism, emphasizing the skill involved.

Sugar Ray Leonard

I love challenges, I love intensity, and I also like to challenge my mind. Believe it or not, boxing is not only about physical force. You use a lot of concentration; it's really mental.

Adriana Lima

Boxing is the toughest and loneliest sport in the world.

Frank Bruno

For some reason, I was drawn towards boxing. Or maybe boxing drew me towards it - because once I put those gloves on, after about six months, boxing was my life.

Sugar Ray Leonard

I made an instant connection with boxing right away. Boxing became such a part of me. I ate boxing, I slept boxing, I lived boxing. Boxing was a way of expressing myself because I was not that outspoken.

Sugar Ray Leonard

I was just such a quiet kid. I found boxing when I was 14 years old. I went down to the gym because my brother, who used to beat me up all the time, introduced me to boxing. I found boxing to be a sport that I felt safe in because I controlled what was in those four squares.

Sugar Ray Leonard

I watched Ali, studied Ali, and I studied Sugar Ray Robinson. I watched them display showmanship. I watched them use pizzazz, personality, and charisma. I took things from them and borrowed things from them because boxing is entertainment.

Sugar Ray Leonard

Without boxing, because of my neighborhoods, who knows what would have happened to me. It was always about following the leader. And I definitely was not a leader. Boxing gave me discipline; a sense of self. It made me more outspoken. It gave me more confidence.

Sugar Ray Leonard

Boxing is fascinating. It's good for the soul to be made to feel clumsy. I swank around during the week thinking I'm a big cheese, but you don't feel like that when you're in the ring with a chap who knows what he's doing. It's ritual humiliation. I'm going to be slugged about and probably killed, but I love it and have to do something to keep fit.

Hugh Laurie

I beat Larry Holmes and George Foreman. I whupped Mike Tyson twice. I had my ear chewed off and spat on the ground in front of me. I've seen everything it is possible to see in boxing. I know this business better than anyone. So I live and die by my own decisions.

Evander Holyfield

I started boxing at 12, and I was above weight for my age, so they put me in the ring with adults... When you're fighting all the time, it gives you the ability to fight without getting angry.

Curtis Jackson

When I was a little kid I wanted to be an artist or a painter. But once I got into boxing, all I wanted was to box.

Emanuel Steward

The trouble with boxing is that too often it ends in sadness.

Barry McGuigan

Although not considered a martial art, boxing is really a martial art. It's a very limited martial art as long as you agree to just box... but in an actual physical fight against someone who's just a wrestler, you're going to get killed.

Joe Rogan

A lot of writers, probably because they're sensitive, which makes them want to be writers, have fears about their masculinity, so they overcompensate by having an interest in boxing and tough-guy things.

Jonathan Ames

I took up boxing out of sheer interest and to help my parents financially.

Mary Kom

Surely, sport is not fundamentally about the safety of athletes. If it were, we'd probably have to ban professional football, right after boxing.

Alice Dreger

Boxing is a buzz, but I went into it to make a living. I wasn't going to go into the ring and get punched in the head for the fun of it.

Frank Bruno

There's not as much oxygen in that hot gym and I think it's great for conditioning. I believe in a lot of boxing. You can train and work on the speed bag and heavy bag, but when you get in the ring with another fighter, it's a different story. Punches are coming at you, there's physical contact, muscle against muscle.

Emanuel Steward

Joe Louis was one of my closest friends.... I'm a great boxing fan. I used to go to the American Legion Stadium in Hollywood, every Friday night for 15 years. Down the aisle would come Lupe Velez, Johnny Weismuller, Mae West. All at ringside.

Mickey Rooney

With experience in boxing, you learn how to be a scientific boxer and how to fight easy.

Manny Pacquiao

I actually study boxing - my dad was a Golden Gloves champion so I learned how to fight at a very young age.

Growing up in Brooklyn you always had to watch your back, so I pretty much learned to protect myself.

Lana Parrilla

Everything I have in this world, I owe to the sport of boxing, and I won't ever forget that.

Oscar De La Hoya

You have a small period of time when you can perfect your career and become good at it. A lot of guys get distracted, which only hurts them. You must stay focused and work very hard at boxing.

Gerry Cooney

Prize-Fighting is not the aim of boxing. This noble exercise ought not to be judged by the dishonesty or the low lives of too many of its professional followers. Let it stand alone, an athletic practice, on the same footing as boating or football.

John Boyle O'Reilly

Unless one is planning to go shopping - basically begging to be smothered by the ravening throngs of returners and bargain hunters; an embrace as constricting as that hugging machine designed by autistic author Temple Grandin - then Boxing Day feels like a bar after last call when the lights have been turned up.

David Rakoff

I took up boxing to get in shape for filming because it's grueling - all the running, the heat, the yelling, the crying that we do.

Steven Yeun

With the advent of chivalry, the art of boxing waned. The evolution of feudal aristocracy, with other and widely different exercises, pastimes and weapons from those of the common people, made boxing unfashionable.

John Boyle O'Reilly

I'd say the most memorable thing for me was my dedication and motivation in how I got so involved in boxing.

Alexis Arguello

The style I have in judo is very unique... One big advantage a judo player has is they have very good posture and - like, wrestlers, they show when they're about to do a take-down... which judo players don't, and so I kind of incorporate the boxing style with a judo grip and finishing that way.

Ronda Rousey

Whatever I lack in size and strength and speed, I kind of make up for in being grittier. When it comes to something like basketball I'm definitely not the best guy on the court, but I love elbowing and pushing people out or boxing them out.

Steven Yeun

Stand-up and boxing are very similar. You're the only one out there, you're going into a fight, and you're going in with a game plan.

Russell Peters

With me, boxing's a beautiful sport.

Nonito Donaire

Politics is comparable to boxing. The only thing is that in politics there are basically no rules. In boxing, you can get a black eye, but in politics you can get poison in your food or a bullet in the head. It's definitely rougher and tougher than other sports.

Wladimir Klitschko

Boxing is a lot of preparation and then improvising, so there are parallels to being an actor.

Seth Numrich

I quit after a bad car accident. The thing about boxing is that you can be a star for five or six years, but when you go back to the old life, it's tough.

Olivier Martinez

The bell that tolls for all in boxing belongs to a cash register.

Bob Verdi

The adoption of gloves for all contests will do more to preserve the practice of boxing than any other conceivable means. It will give pugilism new life, not only as a professional boxer's art, but as a general exercise.

John Boyle O'Reilly

It's not just the physical aspect of boxing, it's the whole fighter mentality that has been ingrained in me through the years as a competitive athlete. One of the hardest things you'll ever do is to box - to get into the ring and to face off with somebody whose whole goal is to knock you out, to hurt you, and to be able to fight back.

Cara Castronuova

Muhammad Ali was the kind of guy you either loved or hated, but you wanted to see him. I happen to really love him. He brought boxing to another level and always made you laugh.

Gerry Cooney

That's the most beautiful thing that I like about boxing: you can take a punch. The biggest thing about taking a punch is your ego reacts and there's no better spiritual lesson than trying to not pay attention to your ego's reaction. That's what takes people out of the fight half the time.

David O. Russell

An incident that left an impression on me was the 1999 sub-junior national boxing championship held in Calcutta. I had trained extremely hard to get there but got kicked out in the first round itself. 'If others can win, why can't you?' I repeatedly asked myself.

Vijender Singh

The first thing I learned in boxing is to not get hit. That's the art of boxing. Execute your opponent without getting hit. In sports school, we were putting our hands behind our backs and having to defend ourselves with our shoulders, by rolling, by moving round the ring, moving out feet.

Wladimir Klitschko

The reality of growing up is we changed schools so many times, my brother was my best friend. We have a five-year age gap, and my brother inspired me. He started boxing, and I just want to show that I could do things better than him.

Wladimir Klitschko

Well I am grooming him, he has a boxing trainer that knows what he is talking about, and once he has that he is able to put everything together and he listens, and when somebody listens they are able to accomplish anything.

Michael Moorer

Sugar Ray Robinson was at the top of the boxing world during the 1950's when it seemed that he would either win or lose the championship about every three or four months.

Dick Schaap

I am much more wired to be an athlete than anything else. I understand the 'hard work = payoff' equation in sports. I run marathons and I box. And that's my Puerto Rican flag hanging in Freddie Roach's Wild Card Boxing gym. I gave it to him. My last N.Y.C. marathon time I ran in three hours flat.

Kirk Acevedo

I lost my edge for boxing, I didn't put as much into it as I did before. I didn't run as far. I didn't train as hard. I didn't eat correctly. I started drinking a little bit every now and then.

Ken Norton

Boxing is really an art form. It might just look like two people beating each other up, but when you look closer, it's actually quite beautiful and interesting.

Seth Numrich

I started athletics in 1999, throwing discus and shot put. I didn't tell my family when I started boxing.

Mary Kom

I love boxing. I box in a local boxing gym in London. I usually spar. But I've done two fights and I lost both of them admirably. I didn't realize how much it would hurt for them to actually hit me.

Oona Chaplin

I always wanted to play a boxer because some of my favorite films, as a boy, were those great boxing movies, like 'Raging Bull', 'Rocky', 'The Set Up', 'Fat City and Hard Times'. I just loved those films.

Holt McCallany

I'm a huge boxing fan. I love the strategy and the combat.

Mark McGrath

Attack is only one half of the art of boxing.

Georges Carpentier

I love boxing. I really respect the guys and admire the guys who do it. But, I'm very, very happy with my career as an actor. I made the right choice and things are really working out for me right now, but I won't pretend that there isn't a part of me that always secretly wanted to be a boxer.

Holt McCallany

I think it's really important to mix cardio with toning, so I love boxing and then add in Pilates or ballet to keep me long and lean and avoid bulking up.

Lily Aldridge

'Rocky' is a movie that just happens to be about boxing. It's really about characters and story lines and relationships and all those things, and the backdrop is boxing. You can go back and watch the final fight in 'Rocky' a thousand times. If you dig that movie, if you like the characters, you'll watch the whole movie over and over.

Triple H

When I was boxing I made five million and wound up broke, owing the government a million.

Joe Louis

I was backstage at the House of Blues in L.A where I was about to perform, and Stevie Wonder and Prince turned up at my dressing room together! Stevie started beat boxing and Prince started singing one of my songs, all of a sudden it was like I was in a cypher with these incredible artists.

Jill Scott

Boxing, mixed martial arts and tennis are the hardest sports to train for.

Andy Murray

I was bullied by a few people who were much older than me. I went to camp to learn boxing. I was 12, and my coach was 24. I felt like if I could fight him, I could stand up to anyone.

Liam Payne

The third man in the ring makes boxing possible.

Joyce Carol Oates

I do shadow boxing and use a heavy bag, but I don't spar with anyone.

Liam Neeson

New York's like a boxing match. In Hollywood, it's like a Fellini movie or something.

John Cusack

I think its so good for boxing when a new guy or new blood as we call it, makes a big statement.

George Foreman

But boxing was my profession. I had to go back the second time because I was broke and I couldn't just go and get a college degree and earn it. I had too many bills, too many families.

George Foreman

I think that every boxer should understand he's on the pedestal for a short span. It's best that you use boxing and don't let boxing use you. Use boxing to sell, because people are selling you through your boxing career, so you have to learn to sell yourself, and you'll never starve.

George Foreman

It would be hard to throw a punch to someone who wasn't a boxer, who wasn't in the ring, and who didn't have on a pair of boxing gloves and who hadn't been training.

George Foreman

Boxing will always be in my life.

Sugar Ray Leonard

Boxing, for me, it's the beginning of all sports. I'm willing to bet that the first sport was a man against another man in a fight, so I think that's something innate in all of us.

Omar Epps

I'd have to say losing the title to Ali in '74 was the lowest moment in sports for me. It was the most devastating thing in my boxing career, and it still hurts to this day.

George Foreman

Oh, there's nothing more dangerous in life at getting hurt at than love itself. People are hurt in love affairs and never recover, more than a boxing match.

George Foreman

I got the script for 'Real Steel.' I started reading and saw that it was about robot boxing, and I was immediately turned off. It's not my thing. But I continued on, and by the time I got to the end of the script, I had chicken skin and tears in my eyes. I thought, 'Man, we don't make movies like this anymore.'

Evangeline Lilly

I didn't excel too highly in school, but I felt that I was moving ahead - and not just in boxing - but in life.

Sugar Ray Leonard

I made the decision to turn pro, and I remember what Ali said to me: 'Get Angelo Dundee. He's the right complexion with the right connection.' He knew boxing. Our relationship was so genuine, so sincere.

Sugar Ray Leonard

A sight game is that I am hurt, but I aim to make you believe I am not even hurt, and with this confidence appearing on my face, I don't panic, otherwise your opponent will know that you are hurt. That's the whole art game in boxing.

Evander Holyfield

They don't show Olympic boxing on TV in prime time. They haven't done that since 1988. In 1992, they showed one: Oscar De La Hoya. In 1996, they didn't show it. In 2000, they didn't show it. In 2004, they didn't show it. In 2008, they did not even mention boxing at all. You would think the United States didn't have a boxing team in 2008.

Evander Holyfield

The game's been good to me and I hope I've been good to the game. I'm 50 years old and I've pretty much did everything that I wanted to do in boxing.

Evander Holyfield

There will always be something about two men in the ring - a mystique because it's pure man-to-man competition. Because of the history boxing has and the tradition it holds, boxing will always have a that mystique.

Sugar Ray Leonard

I knew real show business from my father, who had been an actor since he left the world of boxing.

James Earl Jones

I know it's politically incorrect but I enjoy things like the kick boxing and cock fighting.

Wilbur Smith

That's the biggest problem with boxing in the United States. They do not promote it like they used to, when it used to be Howard Cosell and they showed it on 'Wide World of Sports.' Everybody knew all the fighters. Everybody was looking forward to the year when the Olympics came on.

Evander Holyfield

In modern American politics, being the right kind of ignorant and entertainingly crazy is like having a big right hand in boxing; you've always got a puncher's chance.

Matt Taibbi

The key to any good sports story is identifying the defining moment. In football games or a boxing match, it's usually pretty obvious. But in golf, sometimes it happens on Thursday. Usually it's Sunday, but guys who don't know the game, they can miss it.

Dan Jenkins

Everything in tennis is so neat and nice but boxing has sport down to its essence; it is very pure and I like that.

Andy Murray

Sorry dude, but we're in a boxing match and you went against your word and tried to make me look weak and stupid in front of 17 million people. That's just not gonna happen.

Dustin Diamond

I have never thought of a full-fledged career in Bollywood because boxing has never left my mind. But you never know.

Vijender Singh

Boxing is smoky halls and kidneys battered until they bleed.

Roger Kahn

For an hour every day, I did something. I was on the elliptical or the treadmill, and if someone asked me to go to a class - whether it was spinning, boxing, yoga, you name it - I went. By the end of the month, I felt so good, I just kept going. I didn't want to lose my momentum.

Molly Sims

The brutalities of a fight with bare hands, the crushed nasal bones, maimed lips, and other disfigurements, which call for the utter abolition of boxing in the interests of humanity, at once disappear when the contestants cover their hands with large, soft-leather gloves.

John Boyle O'Reilly

See, I respect boxing because it has given me so much and that's why I will never allow anyone to mistreat the sport of boxing if I can help it.

Alexis Arguello

The entire existence of the NFL - and of football at any level, for all of that - rests on whether or not the game can keep fooling itself, and its paying fan base, that it is somehow superior to boxing and to the rest of our modern blood sports.

Charlie Pierce

Handball, swimming, running, jumping, basketball, and boxing were as much a part of me as breathing.

Gene Tunney

My own ambition in the ring had always been skillful boxing, speed and defense - on the order of Mike Gibbons.

Gene Tunney

Never eat less than four hours before boxing. Then eat only lightly.

Gene Tunney

When you meet someone, ask about what hobby they have, not what they do. People always ask me about cooking, but I prefer to talk about tennis or boxing.

Wolfgang Puck

I think we have tremendous media covering the sport of boxing, even if boxing is a little bit lost in popularity with MMA sports. And I think that with the show 'Lights Out' it's going to get more attention to the sport, and it's going to put more attention to the problems that athletes in general have.

Wladimir Klitschko

Some people who love boxing might love Mike Tyson, but people outside of the sport are generally repulsed by him and therefore, repulsed by the sport.

Dick Schaap

When I got cast in 'Rocky IV,' I had never seen a film camera before. And here I was in this boxing movie.

Dolph Lundgren

In those days, boxing was very glamorous and romantic. You listened to fights on the radio, and a good announcer made it seem like a contest between gladiators.

Joseph Barbera

I didn't push Cory. I wanted him to decide if he wanted to go into boxing and he did. Can't blame it on me.

Leon Spinks

Every boy in a free country ought to be instructed in boxing, wrestling, and the use of weapons. Every young man ought to be drilled. Every householder ought, at least, to have a right to own a rifle, and should know how to make cartridges.

John Boyle O'Reilly

I think when people twitter 20 or 30 times per day, that's too much. They are boxing everyone else out, and people stop following them because they need a break.

Biz Stone

Boxing was not the sport that I thought is was due to all the politics.

Gerry Cooney

With kangaroos, you say 'Sit!' and they start boxing with you. They're nuts!

Jerry O'Connell

I had many boxing matches with my brother in the backyard when we were younger, and I guess while other people abhor boxing for its brutality, I also have to admire anyone who climbs into the ring to face up to what could be the ultimate defeat.

Markus Zusak

If you think you're in shape, try boxing. You'll discover that you are not. It's the most physically challenging thing I've ever attempted, but I love it and I want to keep up some of the training.

Seth Numrich

I've been boxing ever since I was 16. I love surprising people who think a short, blond girl can't fight! Just because I look a certain way doesn't mean I'm weak.

Brittany Snow

I'm probably better known for boxing with Hemingway than for anything I've written.

Morley Callaghan

When I walk for a designer, I walk the ramp as Vijender Singh, the boxer. I believe that by doing so, boxing will at least, in some way, get promoted in our entertainment industry. Plus, if cricketers can, why can't I?

Vijender Singh

As much as I love boxing, I hate it. And as much as I hate it, I love it.

Budd Schulberg

I somewhere along the way became fascinated with exploring characters who are willing to put themselves into violent situations, whether it's football, hockey, boxing, being a cop, being a soldier. There's not a lot of people who are willing to put themselves into those situations.

Peter Berg

At noon I get to the gym to do my boxing workout. Three hours there. Rest. Once in a while I get a massage, because I need it once in while.

Juan Manuel Marquez

I started boxing when I was eight. I enjoyed when I could hit someone and they couldn't hit me back. It was like a game for me. The feeling of knocking someone out. My first knockout victory was when I was ten. He went down and his nose started to bleed, so they stopped it.

Emanuel Steward

You look at boxing being an international, world-famous sport, right up there next with soccer, and there's only two fighters the people want to see fight. Two little fellows, Manny Pacquiao and Floyd Mayweather.

Emanuel Steward

Fighting is dancing. Look at a great boxing match, and it's a dancing.

David Lyons

I'm a huge boxing and mixed martial arts fan.

Sung Hi Lee

One thing I like about boxing is that I will not have to deal with the same kind of politics that I had to in skating. In boxing, it is not about your appearance, or how your costume looks, what color it is, or how much it costs.

Tonya Harding

I don't watch TV dramas. I watch ESPN, HBO boxing, National Geographic Channel and I kind of like to get some DVDs, movies that I haven't seen and I just pop them in.

Dominic Purcell

To be the first Puerto Rican to win a world title in four divisions would be an achievement. Gomez, Benitez, there have been a lot of good fighters from Puerto Rico before me. When I started boxing, Tito Trinidad was our big star.

Miguel Cotto

Sexy boxing is something that takes away from the brutality of boxing.

Mark de Mori

I was always active, always running and working out. I was a wrestler and ran track and, out of interest, started boxing. It's always been a part of me.

T. J. Thyne

I grew up in Westlake Villiage, a suburb of L.A. There was a guy there who was a fighter and was like, 'I'll teach you to box.' I started a little bit of boxing, then it crossed over into jiu-jitsu. I was into it for a little while, but then I started doing basketball, baseball, team sports.

Jonathan Lipnicki

If people recognize me from 'The Vampire Diaries,' they just give me that look that's like, 'I think I know you. I think I saw you boxing in 1912, but I'm not sure,' because it was such a short-lived run.

Cassidy Freeman

But if you cover the World Series on the news or do a feature on an Ali boxing match then all of a sudden ears go up all over the place and people say what the hell are you doing. The reason for that is that we're doing something that people are really interested in.

Roone Arledge

Boxing is always serious.

Juan Manuel Marquez

I do actually use a boxing trainer when I train for stand-up.

Louis C. K.

In boxing, you don't know what's going to happen. In wrestling, it's already prearranged.

Mickey Rourke

What I know about Mike Tyson, I see in the boxing ring. As far as all of the gossip stuff that I hear about him, I know first hand to take that with a grain of salt.

Gerald McRaney

I love boxing, and boxing has always been my favorite sport. I was always into it, and I boxed recreationally all of my life.

Holt McCallany

I don't like any sport except boxing and bull fighting.

David Bailey

And I love kick boxing. It's a lot of fun. It gives you a lot of confidence when you can kick somebody in the head.

Alicia Keys

I like boxing movies. One of the hardest things for me to watch as far as boxing films, is the boxing. The actual boxing usually sucks.

Omar Epps

The integration of a headgear in professional boxing would do so much to make it safer for young men. They could go into the sport, make a lot of money and then come out and be good grandfathers.

George Foreman

I land a higher percentage of punches than any boxer in boxing.

Floyd Mayweather, Jr.

www.ingramcontent.com/pod-product-compliance
Lightning Source LLC
Chambersburg PA
CBHW071114280526
45787CB00003B/1032